CLARINET

ALL I ASK	2
CHASING PAVEMENTS	4
HELLO	6
MAKE YOU FEEL MY LOVE	8
MILLION YEARS AGO	9
REMEDY	10
ROLLING IN THE DEEP	12
RUMOUR HAS IT	14
SET FIRE TO THE RAIN	16
SKYFALL	21
SOMEONE LIKE YOU	18
WHEN WE WERE YOUNG	22

To access audio visit:
www.halleonard.com/mylibrary

Enter Code
7998-6794-7736-9973

ISBN 978-1-4950-6296-4

Cover photo © dpa picture alliance / Alamy Stock Photo

HAL•LEONARD®
CORPORATION
7777 W. BLUEMOUND RD. P.O. BOX 13819 MILWAUKEE, WI 53213

Visit Hal Leonard Online at
www.halleonard.com

ALL I ASK

CLARINET

Words and Music by ADELE ADKINS,
PHILIP LAWRENCE, BRUNO MARS
and CHRIS BROWN

3

To Coda ⊕   D.S. al Coda   CODA ⊕

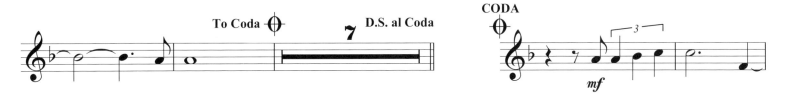

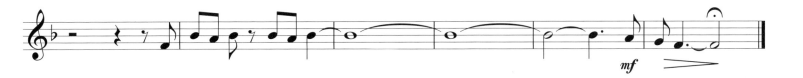

CHASING PAVEMENTS

CLARINET

Words and Music by ADELE ADKINS
and FRANCIS EG WHITE

5

HELLO

CLARINET

Words and Music by ADELE ADKINS
and GREG KURSTIN

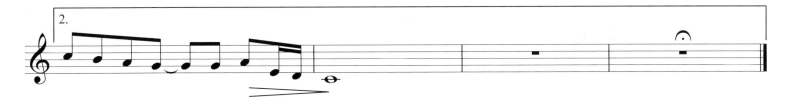

MAKE YOU FEEL MY LOVE

CLARINET

Words and Music by
BOB DYLAN

Moderately, with feeling

MILLION YEARS AGO

Clarinet

Words and Music by ADELE ADKINS
and GREGORY KURSTIN

REMEDY

CLARINET

Words and Music by ADELE ADKINS
and RYAN TEDDER

ROLLING IN THE DEEP

CLARINET

Words and Music by ADELE ADKINS
and PAUL EPWORTH

RUMOUR HAS IT

CLARINET

Words and Music by ADELE ADKINS
and RYAN TEDDER

SET FIRE TO THE RAIN

CLARINET

Words and Music by ADELE ADKINS
and FRASER SMITH

SOMEONE LIKE YOU

CLARINET

Words and Music by ADELE ADKINS
and DAN WILSON

SKYFALL

from the Motion Picture SKYFALL

Clarinet

Words and Music by ADELE ADKINS
and PAUL EPWORTH

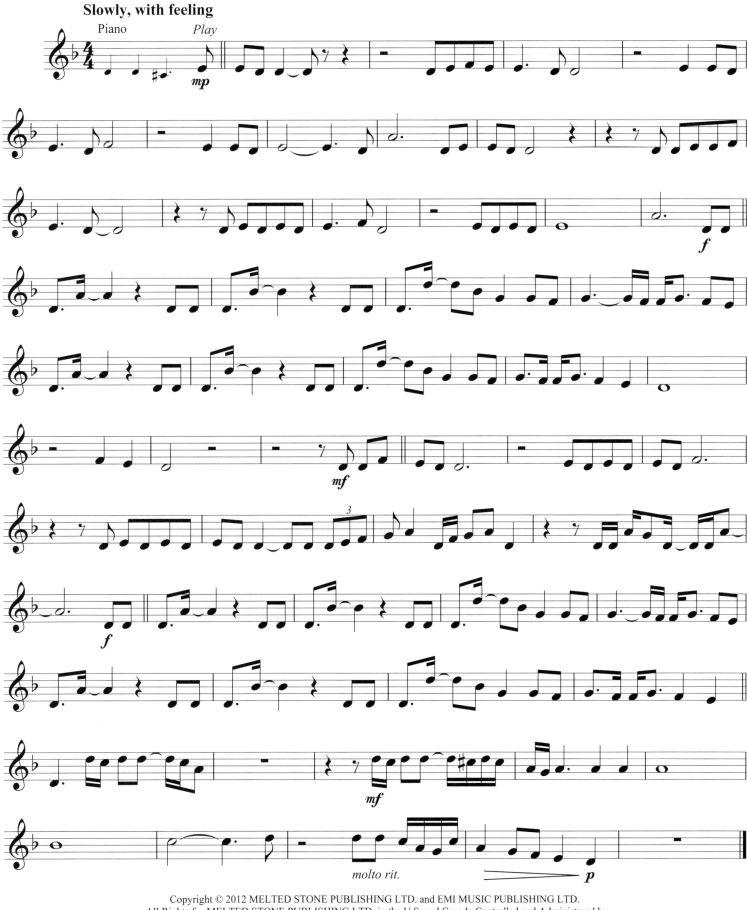

WHEN WE WERE YOUNG

CLARINET

Words and Music by ADELE ADKINS
and TOBIAS JESSO JR.

Slowly, soulfully

Chart Hits

All About That Bass • All of Me • Happy • Radioactive • Roar • Say Something • Shake It Off • A Sky Full of Stars • Someone like You • Stay with Me • Thinking Out Loud • Uptown Funk.

_____	00146207	Flute	$12.99
_____	00146208	Clarinet	$12.99
_____	00146209	Alto Sax	$12.99
_____	00146210	Tenor Sax	$12.99
_____	00146211	Trumpet	$12.99
_____	00146212	Horn	$12.99
_____	00146213	Trombone	$12.99
_____	00146214	Violin	$12.99
_____	00146215	Viola	$12.99
_____	00146216	Cello	$12.99

Coldplay

Clocks • Every Teardrop Is a Waterfall • Fix You • In My Place • Lost! • Paradise • The Scientist • Speed of Sound • Trouble • Violet Hill • Viva La Vida • Yellow.

_____	00103337	Flute	$12.99
_____	00103338	Clarinet	$12.99
_____	00103339	Alto Sax	$12.99
_____	00103340	Tenor Sax	$12.99
_____	00103341	Trumpet	$12.99
_____	00103342	Horn	$12.99
_____	00103343	Trombone	$12.99
_____	00103344	Violin	$12.99
_____	00103345	Viola	$12.99
_____	00103346	Cello	$12.99

Disney Greats

Arabian Nights • Hawaiian Roller Coaster Ride • It's a Small World • Look Through My Eyes • Yo Ho (A Pirate's Life for Me) • and more.

_____	00841934	Flute	$12.99
_____	00841935	Clarinet	$12.99
_____	00841936	Alto Sax	$12.99
_____	00841937	Tenor Sax	$12.95
_____	00841938	Trumpet	$12.95
_____	00841939	Horn	$12.95
_____	00841940	Trombone	$12.95
_____	00841941	Violin	$12.99
_____	00841942	Viola	$12.95
_____	00841943	Cello	$12.95
_____	00842078	Oboe	$12.99

Great Themes

Bella's Lullaby • Chariots of Fire • Get Smart • Hawaii Five-O Theme • I Love Lucy • The Odd Couple • Spanish Flea • and more.

_____	00842468	Flute	$12.99
_____	00842469	Clarinet	$12.99
_____	00842470	Alto Sax	$12.99
_____	00842471	Tenor Sax	$12.99
_____	00842472	Trumpet	$12.99
_____	00842473	Horn	$12.99
_____	00842474	Trombone	$12.99
_____	00842475	Violin	$12.99
_____	00842476	Viola	$12.99
_____	00842477	Cello	$12.99

Lennon & McCartney Favorites

All You Need Is Love • A Hard Day's Night • Here, There and Everywhere • Hey Jude • Let It Be • Nowhere Man • Penny Lane • She Loves You • When I'm Sixty-Four • and more.

_____	00842600	Flute	$12.99
_____	00842601	Clarinet	$12.99
_____	00842602	Alto Sax	$12.99
_____	00842603	Tenor Sax	$12.99
_____	00842604	Trumpet	$12.99
_____	00842605	Horn	$12.99
_____	00842606	Trombone	$12.99
_____	00842607	Violin	$12.99
_____	00842608	Viola	$12.99
_____	00842609	Cello	$12.99

Popular Hits

Breakeven • Fireflies • Halo • Hey, Soul Sister • I Gotta Feeling • I'm Yours • Need You Now • Poker Face • Viva La Vida • You Belong with Me • and more.

_____	00842511	Flute	$12.99
_____	00842512	Clarinet	$12.99
_____	00842513	Alto Sax	$12.99
_____	00842514	Tenor Sax	$12.99
_____	00842515	Trumpet	$12.99
_____	00842516	Horn	$12.99
_____	00842517	Trombone	$12.99
_____	00842518	Violin	$12.99
_____	00842519	Viola	$12.99
_____	00842520	Cello	$12.99

Songs from Frozen, Tangled and Enchanted

Do You Want to Build a Snowman? • For the First Time in Forever • Happy Working Song • I See the Light • In Summer • Let It Go • Mother Knows Best • That's How You Know • True Love's First Kiss • When Will My Life Begin • and more.

_____	00126921	Flute	$12.99
_____	00126922	Clarinet	$12.99
_____	00126923	Alto Sax	$12.99
_____	00126924	Tenor Sax	$12.99
_____	00126925	Trumpet	$12.99
_____	00126926	Horn	$12.99
_____	00126927	Trombone	$12.99
_____	00126928	Violin	$12.99
_____	00126929	Viola	$12.99
_____	00126930	Cello	$12.99

Women of Pop

Bad Romance • Jar of Hearts • Mean • My Life Would Suck Without You • Our Song • Rolling in the Deep • Single Ladies (Put a Ring on It) • Teenage Dream • and more.

_____	00842650	Flute	$12.99
_____	00842651	Clarinet	$12.99
_____	00842652	Alto Sax	$12.99
_____	00842653	Tenor Sax	$12.99
_____	00842654	Trumpet	$12.99
_____	00842655	Horn	$12.99
_____	00842656	Trombone	$12.99
_____	00842657	Violin	$12.99
_____	00842658	Viola	$12.99
_____	00842659	Cello	$12.99

Wicked

As Long As You're Mine • Dancing Through Life • Defying Gravity • For Good • I'm Not That Girl • Popular • The Wizard and I • and more.

_____	00842236	Flute	$11.95
_____	00842237	Clarinet	$11.99
_____	00842238	Alto Saxophone	$11.99
_____	00842239	Tenor Saxophone	$11.95
_____	00842240	Trumpet	$11.99
_____	00842241	Horn	$11.95
_____	00842242	Trombone	$11.95
_____	00842243	Violin	$11.95
_____	00842244	Viola	$11.95
_____	00842245	Cello	$11.95

FOR MORE INFORMATION, SEE YOUR LOCAL MUSIC DEALER, OR WRITE TO:

HAL•LEONARD® CORPORATION

7777 W. BLUEMOUND RD. P.O. BOX 13819 MILWAUKEE, WI 53213

Prices, contents, and availability subject to change without notice.
Disney characters and artwork © Disney Enterprises, Inc.

0116